# TITILLATING TALES
## *from the*
# OUTHOUSE

### AND OTHER PERKY POETIC ADVENTURES

## TOM LEECH

Copyright © 2024 Tom Leech.

All rights reserved. No part of this book may be reproduced, stored, or transmitted by any means—whether auditory, graphic, mechanical, or electronic—without written permission of both publisher and author, except in the case of brief excerpts used in critical articles and reviews. Unauthorized reproduction of any part of this work is illegal and is punishable by law.

ISBN: 979-8-89419-497-4 (sc)
ISBN: 979-8-89419-498-1 (hc)
ISBN: 979-8-89419-499-8 (e)

Because of the dynamic nature of the Internet, any web addresses or links contained in this book may have changed since publication and may no longer be valid. The views expressed in this work are solely those of the author and do not necessarily reflect the views of the publisher, and the publisher hereby disclaims any responsibility for them.

One Galleria Blvd., Suite 1900, Metairie, LA 70001
(504) 702-6708

# CONTENTS

What Some Outhouse Fans are Saying About this Book ................ix
Outhouses? ..........................................................................................xi
Books By Tom Leech ........................................................................xii
Preface ...............................................................................................xiii

**Titillating Tales from the Outhouse** ............................................... 1
1. Ode To Sir Thomas .......................................................................2
2. Jose, The Frontier Capitalist .......................................................4

**The Gourmet** ..................................................................................... 7
3. Tale of the Three Outhouse Tippers ...........................................8
4. Outhouses In Winter. Gee, What Fun! ....................................12

**Music Man** ........................................................................................15
5. Ode to a Titian Urn ...................................................................17
6. Where's the Outhouse? .............................................................21

**Priorities** ......................................................................................... 23
7. On the Move With the Road Gang ..........................................24
8. Quandary in the Campground .................................................28
9. Two Women on the Move .........................................................31
10. You Don't Want to be there When the Black Water Blows ........33
11. Joey Takes a Nose Dive ............................................................37
12. Rodney Drops the Goods ........................................................40

**The Usual** .................................................................. 43
13. Outhouse Blues ........................................... 44
14. Getting Straight Poop for Those Special Seats ........................47
15. My Kingdom for a Seat ........................................50
16. Duck & Cover ........................................................53
17. Skip to My...Whahhh??? ................................................56
18. When You Get the Clue, What're You Gonna' Do? ................58
19. The Outhouse That Pooped Out ................................................61
20. Big Buns Stuck Up There ................................................64

**A Key Query** ........................................................................ 67
21. Where Does Santa Go? ..............................................................68

**Other Spicy Tale** ........................................................ 71
1. Is There Any Hope? ..............................................................72

**A Place To P(Lan?)** ........................................................ 75
2. The Legend of Emily Morgan, The Heroine of San Jacinto ..........76
3. KC at the Bar ..............................................................80
4. Saturday Bath on the Farm ........................................83
5. I Never Peed in the Pool ........................................85
6. Trouble at the Market ........................................87
7. How Sweet the Air... Gasp, Cough, Aghhh ........................90

**Capone** ........................................................................ 93
8. Guys Don't Peek ..............................................................94

**Back to the Outhouse** ........................................................ 97
1. The Passing of the Backhouse ........................................98
2. The Three Bares ........................................101
3. Toilet Seats ........................................104

**William Shakespeare** ..................................................................107
1. The Bard Heads for the Privy ....................................................108

**For Those Who Want to Sit and Think** ...................................113
Some Classic Outhouse Gems ........................................................ 115
More Current Outhouse Dandies.................................................... 116
Even More Outhouse Events and Places ......................................... 119

Here's Space For Your Poetic Notes ...............................................120
About Tom Leech ........................................................................ 121
Afterword.....................................................................................123

# WHAT SOME OUTHOUSE FANS ARE SAYING ABOUT THIS BOOK

"A delightful read! If ever there was a reason to praise the outdoor privy, Leech's anthology of clever quips, quotes, poems and dirty little ditties sets the standard!"
M. Lee Buompensiero, award-winner author of *Sumerland*

"I got chuckles galore from your clever well-spiced rhymes. Your outhouse tales will stir lots of fun memories for many of us who've had ample experience with those little casas out back."
Art Banta, author of *King Arthur and His Ribald (K)nights*

"A whimsical journey to a different kind of netherworld. Naughty fun!"
Gered Beeby, author of *Dark Option*

"As a young Indiana farm boy, I have fond memories of the old outhouse we had on our family farm in the 40's & 50's with its Sears Roebuck catalog—and some not-so-fond memories. Looking forward to seeing Tom's completed collection of stories & poems."
Tom Smith, Indiana Educator- Farm Boy

"Who knew the loo was a locale for lyricism? Author Leech plumbs the privy for lively limericks that will keep you tickled while you while away the minutes—or hours. An absorbing diversion for one and all."
PJ Adams, author of *Freud's Revenge* and *Intoxicating Paris*

"Never in my life did I realize there was so much to say about outhouses! From drunken damsels to a triad of escaped convicts to the outhouse adventures of Santa Claus, this book of poems is a delight. It transports the reader to another time and (odorous) place in a deluge of hysterical whimsy. I challenge you not to giggle."
Sondra Thiederman, Ph.D., Professional Speaker and Author of *3 Keys to Defeating Unconscious Bias: Watch, Think, Act*

"Limericks have long been a treasured art form, and Tom Leech's new book brings the most ordinary events in life into focus in *Titillating Tales from the Outhouse*. Leech, a California writer whose roots are in rural Indiana, rhymes and riffs in the great tradition of Ogden Nash or even William Shakespeare. Delightfully funny."
Phil Oakley, author of *The Morello Family: Pin Raids* and *Telegraph*

# OUTHOUSES?

## WHAT'S THIS ABOUT?

Welcome readers. This is a book of humorous poetic tales related to the subject of the outhouse. I grew up in a small Midwestern town and had many relatives who lived on nearby farms. Most did not have indoor plumbing, so the outhouse, was a constant source of humor, day and night, summer and winter. For campers, world travelers, and people with powerful memories, outhouses, johns, WCs, toilettes, crappers, two-holers, los baños…continue to be a topic of amusement.

So here you'll read

- Original poems, many tweaked by my personal experiences, all addressing some whacky outhouse story or dilemma;
- More original poems, not outhouse, but in the same general concept—humor, having fun with language, spicy;
- Classic outhouse poems written by several legendary story tellers.

So, jump in there and have fun with these titillating tales

# BOOKS BY TOM LEECH

(A VERSATILE AUTHOR)

*Fun on the Job: Amusing and true tales from Rosie-the Riveters to Rocket Scientists at a Major Aerospace Company*
Presentations Press, 2017

*How to Prepare, Stage & Deliver Winning Presentations, 3rd Edition*
AMACOM American Management Association) 2004

*Say it like Shakespeare: The Bard's Timeless Tips for Communication Success* 2nd **Ed.**
Presentations Press 2013 (Previously published in 2001 by McGraw-Hill)

*The Curious Adventures of Santa's Wayward Elves*
with Leslie Johnson-Leech, Presentations Press 2014

*On the Road in '68: a year of turmoil, a journey of friendship*
Presentations Press 2009.

*Outdoors San Diego: Hiking, Biking and* **Camping**
with Jack Farnan, Premier 2004

# PREFACE

This book is the result of many poems and anecdotes written over the years. I've bounced these off many of my cronies, all of whom have had similar early years to mine. That is, they have had many early experiences with outhouses and the humor that has been a large part of that necessity of heading out to the little shack outback. I've been encouraged to keep writing more of these humorous odes by their responses. Among those pals, departed too early are Roger, Bwana, Strain, multi-Toms, Clyde/Mar, and several Bills (including my brother). Others who recall outhouses well are cronies and kinfolk from those early countryside days: Phil, Duane, Mont, Karen, Chief, Ferg, Len, Clayt, Whitey, and more. Then some more current chums chuckle at the subject, including Carolyn, Warren, Marcia, Vikky, Dan, Socrates, multi-Pats, Mary & Steve, Skip…

Also, this finished product was helped significantly by several fellow scribblers (check the previous section of Outhouse Fans); wife, fellow author, and detailed reviewer/error-catcher Leslie; and the skillful and patient editor Rick Lakin who did the detailed work required to get an actual book created. Thank you all.

# TITILLATING TALES
## —— *from the* ——
# OUTHOUSE

*Footoo/Shutterstock.com*

# 1. ODE TO SIR THOMAS

## WHO FOUND A NEED AND FILLED IT

*Those little shacks outback go by many names – outhouses,
privies, porta-potties, johns, cans, thrones, and more in other languages.*

A rock-solid axiom for entrepreneurs,
As they look for a way to get rich,
Is above all you must have a real market,
One that creates its own special niche.

Don't invent something just 'cause you like it,
Or your baby sister thinks it's cute.
But do find a product that fills a need,
Especially one that's major to boot.

So first do some serious thinking,
'Bout what people do from morning to night.
Sure' what they <u>like</u> to do is good,
But what they <u>must</u> do's where you aim your sight.

And that's what made the bell ring for Sir Thomas,
When he saw something that all had to do,
(While he was thinking out back in the privy)
And that "doing" was at home, shop or zoo.

"Aha!" he shouted, "I sense here a true need,"
(His mind worked well when in a restful mood,
Though not so good seated out there in winter)
"What can I create that won't get me booed?"

"This shack we sit in works fine in July,
Though complaints abound from both gent or lady,
But in December going outside's no fun,
What might work better for Roscoe or Sadie?"

"That pot under the bed is somewhat a fix,
Keeps us from freezing out there in the rain,
But one flaw's with the products still there below,
Pitching it come morning sure is a pain.

"What about that pipe bringing water inside?
Can't we use that to haul our stuff out?
That way we can each do our thing in the house,
While list'ning to the news of last night's bout.

So, Sir Thomas put his skills toward a fix,
A gadget <u>inside</u> that well met nature's calls.
Some said it wiped out the old shack's romance,
But soon it was there in schools, houses, and malls.

Some consumers had to be nurtured a bit,
With some saying they felt like a sinner.
But one sit-down demo showed its true value,
Soon all agreed, "Sir Tom's got a winner!"

But what to call it was the next big issue,
"It needs a fine label, something really dapper,
"How 'bout we name it after the designer?"
And that's where we got it - from Sir Thomas Crapper.

# 2. JOSE, THE FRONTIER CAPITALIST

## (EL BAÑO MERCADO DE LA FRONTERA)

*The border crossing from Tijuana, Mexico, to San Diego, California, is the busiest in the world. Much of that is due to business and much related to people crossing the border for a good time, such as the couple in this tale.*

On a lovely Sunday in Tijuana, Mexico,
A trip below the border for Jack and Joan,
It had been a lively day for the two of them,
Having some fun on Ave Revolución.

At Rosita's cantina, they'd had a few cervezas,
And yummy enchiladas made to order.
Time to head the Chevy north and back to El Cajon.
"Let's wrap up the day and head for the border."

"Ay chihuahua!" said Jack when he saw cars galore
Ten blocks from the frontier and at a slow creep,
At least two hours to make it across the border.
"Glad you're driving," murmured Joan, nearly asleep.

A half-hour later, it appeared they'd barely moved.
"Those beers," said Jack, "are making me trotty,
"Wonder if there's a handy restroom somewhere 'round here.
"Well, look at that, a good old porta-potty."

EL BANO BUENO - said the sign - ONLY ONE DOLLAR.
"What?" moaned Jack. "A buck to pee? No way, Jose!"
"A sus ordones," said the vendor, a real Jose,
"Fat chance," avowed Jack, "You won't rob me today."

A half-hour more and still a whole mess of traffic,
"Hmm," thought Jack, "This may be heading toward some grief,
"Where's that crook Jose and his gol-darned porta potty?
"Let's pay his two bucks; I could use some relief."

Soon another showed, and there once more that same Jose.
"Hooray," shouted Jack (and Joan echoed, "Good thing!").
Jose had his money belt ready for dinero.
"Here's two bucks—open up, we'll give it a fling"

"Welcome," said Jose. "Here it is at your disposal.
"And the fee now is only five dollars each."
"What?" screamed Jack, feeling more than a trifle
puckery, "It was one buck–five's a contractual breach!"

"You're a bandit," Jack groaned, and his bladder did the same.
"I'll complain to the Better Business Bureaus."
Said Jose, with a grin, "No problema—manana,
"But the price is five, and yes, we take Euros."

"It's highway robbery!" said Jack, "For that, I'll just hold it."
So on they went, but the line just stayed right there.
"I've got to go now!" shrieked Jack, and Joan moaned, "Amen."
Now squirming in their seats was this twitchy pair.

"Where's that Jose and his EL BANO OUTRAGIOSO?"
And Jose, with one more outhouse, did appear.
"Here's our five bucks each. Unlock that door, muy pronto!"
"But senor," said Jose, "the price is ten here."

"What? First one buck, then five, and now you're charging us ten!
"You crook, preying on our now desperate need."
"Ah, si," said Jose, with an accommodating smile.
"We're like gringos–fill a need, enjoy the greed."

"Are your needs not more pressing from when you joined the line?"
"Here's 20!" said Jack, darting from the Chevy.
"Welcome, it's yours," said Jose, opening the door,
As Jack and Joan raced headlong for the privy.

Now at the border, the guard gave them a friendly grin,
Checking the Chevy's seats, trunk, and all the rest.
"I see you're a Jose customer. That's fine with us.
We're his partners—free enterprise at its best."

*Note: This poem was triggered by my many trips heading back across the border from Tijuana to my home base of San Diego. Since this was written a few decades ago, the wait times to get vehicles back across the border have grown longer, so the possibility of Jose's enterprise finding success has likely increased.*

# THE GOURMET

There once was a gourmet named Jack, Bean burritos were his favorite snack, He'd gobble them up all day, But there was a price to pay, As he'd dash to that little house out back.

*By Elya - Own work, CC BY-SA 3.0,
https://commons.wikimedia.org/w/index.php?curid=15203868*

# 3. TALE OF THE THREE OUTHOUSE TIPPERS

*In many country communities, Halloween often sees local rascals scouting out those little houses that might be ripe for messing with. Here's a frequent result.*

They oft-heard cheers as the Three Musketeers,
Harry, Joe, and Twirly they were named,
A trio of wanks who loved to pull pranks,
And hooted aloud when others got blamed.

When folks came back from a night on the town,
And saw their house well-covered with TP,
Most of the time their fingers were pointed,
In the direction of that rowdy three.

When the principal's car turned up on blocks,
No one squealed, tho several did snicker,
And odds were that the trio'd been working,
Maybe inspired by a bit of likker.

Once some ripe melons were gone from the patch.
And some wondered who'd done these new sins.
Could it be those three looking like angels,
With melon juice dripping down their chins?

Then came Halloween—too much to resist,
Got to stir up some fuss and alarm.
So they looked 'round for ways to cause trouble,
While they cavorted through field and farm.

Well, what's this, such an intriguing structure?
Now creeping as quiet as a mouse,
They headed over toward that small, lone shack,
Which sat there by Farmer Jake's house.

Slowly they eased through the bushes and trees,
To that prime invitation in back,
A few more steps, then a good solid heave,
And, hee, hee, over would go that shack.

Except Farmer Jake was not a sucker,
And his outhouse had been tipped before.
So, on this year he was out for revenge,
Yes, determined to even the score.

So, he'd rigged his shack to a sneaky track,
So, he could slide the privy away,
Then covered the open pit with branches,
His privy was now ready for play.

Sure enough, here came the stealthy trio,
Tiptoeing softly across the clover.
"Looks pretty nifty, and no one's around,
We'll just grab it and pitch it on over."

Then <u>swoosh</u> they flew right down into the stew,
"Oh, my gawd!!" Came the shrieks from the three,
"It's a sloppy bin, and it's goop we're in!"
As they thrashed midst the sludge and the sea.

They flailed and they sunk, and especially they stunk,
As they tried desperately to retreat,
'Til, at last, they clambered up and on out,
And again felt real ground 'neath their feet.

Toward home, they did slink, with their woeful
stink, When some cronies rode by on their bikes,
"My, my! What's that stench?" came their taunting
snorts, "Are the Musketeers out for some hikes?"

From then on the threesome had new names,
Borrowed from the screen's famed blundering pack
They were now Larry, Moe, and Curly,
"Smell that, guys? Our own three stooges are back."

And Farmer Jake was the toast of the burg,
As he told of the floppers' sad wails
And his farmer pals howled loud with laughter,
As they fitted their own shacks with rails.

*Carol M. Highsmith, Photographer*

# 4. OUTHOUSES IN WINTER. GEE, WHAT FUN!

*When you live in winter climates, going to the outhouse is a very different experience from summer, but…nature insists.*

If there was one thing we kids'd dread,
That's when out to that back shack we'd head,
And the calendar showed winter as the season
And when hittin' the can was the reason.

So, when the urge said get out there and dash,
Even tho we hadn't et all of our hash,
We'd peek outside for a wary look,
Then grab a jacket from the hook.

Next, shove our feet into the boots,
You'd likely need 'em for most of the routes,
Put on some mitts and pull on a hat,
And give a shove to the lazy cat.

Can't delay any longer, quit the bitchin'—
Push open that door off the kitchen,
First, test the air before headin' out,
Come on get movin', you wimpy lout!

So enuf of those nervous twitches,
Go, unless you want some soiled britches,
Trek carefully though, be a bit discrete
Along that path, filled with snow and sleet.

Now another task at the little hut,
Damned entry door is frozen shut,
Use that shovel to scrape away the ice,
Might even wake up the spiders and mice.

Starting to freeze so don't stop to tweet,
Drop your drawers and have yourself a seat,
Oh Lordy, that seat's covered with frost,
Yes, I could sit on it, but what'll be the cost?

Now a reminder of something sad,
Why didn't I bring along that furry pad?
Too late now so down I plop,
Ay Chihuahua! It's a frozen flop!

Certainly not now the time nor nook
To peruse my usual comic book,
Just shiver along and take care of biz,
Whether it's #2 or just a whiz.

Still more to do despite the nasty weather,
Sears cat'log's no good, pages stuck together,
Grab the newspaper, stem the dike,
With the pic of the candidate, you don't like.

Now back on that path right up to the house,
Brrr, let me in, cuz, forget I'm a louse!
Let that wood-fired stove warm my frame,
And toward Granny's hot cider, I'll swiftly aim.

Pa and the uncles are playin' euchre,
Munchin' popcorn for some tasty lucre,
I'm still shiverin'—that trip was a bummer,
So, when nature calls, can't it wait 'til summer?

# MUSIC MAN

A chap who'd made bucks as a trapper,
Tried a new career as a rapper,
He'd jot down his cool beats,
On those Sears Roebuck sheets,
Thus his lyrics bloomed in the crapper.

# BRRRRR….. WHY AM I TAKING SO LONG?

*Ermal Oksana/Shutterstock.com*

# 5. ODE TO A TITIAN URN
## OR LET'S HEAR IT FOR THE CHAMBERPOT

*Well, there was one useful solution to performing in winter.*

At Grandma's, as the day moved to a close,
The kids of the clan headed up to bed,
The females took the bedroom to the right,
The left for Jake and me and cousin Fred.

Grandma and Grandpa had their room downstairs,
and Uncle Ralph got the room by the back.
We'd had supper, played Hearts, War, or
Euchre, Now we all were ready to hit the sack.

You could hear the wind whistlin' outside.
Brrr, it was winter in Indiany,
Thank goodness we had these warm covers,
Without them, for sure, you'd freeze your fanny.

For awhile we told jokes and scary stories,
And listened to giggling from across the hall,
But it wasn't long before our eyelids drooped,
Then it was just snoozing by one and all.

But then a bit later one of us'd stir–
It was nature's call – now who had to go?
You'd mull it over and think maybe not you,
But soon, the need really would let you know.

Now Grandma's farmhouse had no plumbing inside.
We knew where the path to the throne room led,
To that little old shack out the kitchen door
A short walk over by the chicken shed.

Brrr, it's freezing here, is that my only choice?
To leave that warm bed, head out into the sleet,
With an old overcoat and pair of galoshes,
Then dash, not walk, out to that ice-cold seat?

No—'cause each room had a chamberpot,
Kept under the bed and always ready.
When the need hit, there was the answer,
Slide it out, then make sure you were steady.

Our pot had a neat painting on the side,
From an artist whose name we'd come to learn;
Mom said he was a famous Italian,
So, of course, we called it our Titian urn.

Nothing was better than that Titian urn.
You did your duty, shoved it 'neath the bed,
And crawled once more under those warm covers,
Then back to dreamsville was where your mind led.

Almost asleep, then comes that sound we know,
From next door, a cousin slips from her sack.
Responding to that same essential call,
Then creaking bed-springs as she heads on back.

Come next morning and good old Uncle Ralph,
Got the pot-bellied stove fired up,
We'd jump out of bed and into some duds,
Slurp some hot chocolate from a cup.

Then one of our chores was to carry our pot,
Over to that little shack by the shed,
And we'd empty the collection from the night,
Scrub it and slide it back under the bed.

Then all day we ignored the chamberpot,
But we knew it surely would get its turn,
When once again as we all hit the sack,
And proclaimed, "Hooray for our Titian urn."

—from 2017 Oasis Journal

*Source: Tom's personal picture files*

# 6. WHERE'S THE OUTHOUSE?

*In most life situations today, the need for an outhouse is not strong. But there often comes a time when you ask…*

So, there you are on an airline's toilet,
And space is so tight that you can barely move,
You say designers need sharper thinking,
Couldn't they see a better way to improve? –
And you proclaim, "Where's the outhouse?"

When you've checked into that Paris hotel,
And it's walk, walk, and walk up to that 6$^{th}$ floor,
Then you plop down onto your room's toilet,
Where the space is so tight, you can't close the door—
Then you mutter, "Where's the outhouse?"

When you're in Bombay, Rome or Peru,
And your innards signal it's time to unload,
And you find the toilet has no seat,
What dingdong, you ask, would build such a commode?
And you holler, "Where's the outhouse?"

When you're out hiking on a long trail,
And nature says no john's about to appear,
So, you find a handy bush and crouch,
Then sharp cactus barbs pierce your newly-bared rear –
Then you shriek, "Where's the outhouse?"

When you're sailing in a hot air balloon,
And last night's ample brews signal an alert.,
That the time's arrived to find quick relief
But what's any option to not wet your skirt? –
Then you moan, "Where's the outhouse?"

True, outhouses are the source of jokes,
Yet porta-potties are all over the place,
While they might impede on nature's view,
They meet that key need, with a real seat and space –
And they answer the query, "Where's the outhouse?

# PRIORITIES

A convict was sent to Cataño,
Whose name was Richie Alejandro,
"Guard, I've got one main concern,
One thing important to learn,
Donde esta that there el baño"

*Fotokon/shutterstock.com*

# 7. ON THE MOVE WITH THE ROAD GANG

*Real News Item: Prisoner on work detail, in trailer porta-potty. Driver wheels away with trailer, up to 40 mph before the driver was alerted.*

They came out in the prison van,
And to their jobs, they went.
To pick up litter was the plan,
To which the prisoners bent.

Bank robber Duke was in the group,
Out by the main highway,
Tossing the trash into his scoop,
So far, a useful day.

When nature called—to Duke it talked—
He signaled trustee Juan.
"I gotta go," then up he stepped,
Into the port-a-john.

The standard yellow was its shade,
Mounted on the trailer,
The scent proclaimed it medium grade,
Basic per the jailer.

Duke took his seat upon the throne,
And hove unto the task.
His colleagues heard a gentle groan,
As Duke in peace did bask.

Up in the cab, the driver stirred,
Move it out, no time to barter,
He stretched and got his eyes unblurred,
And turned on the starter.

Away he went onto the road,
With trailer now in tow,
He did not note an extra load,
One passenger to go.

Duke shook awake in his small hut.
"Now what the heck is this?"
A sudden splash on his bare butt,
Then "Hey, stop, whoa, desist!"

The driver moved on through the gears,
With each a jolting lurch.
Duke tightly hung on, in arrears,
To keep his precious perch.

He tried to stand to make a thump,
But moving was no snap.
His pants were down and with each bump,
That wet stuff went, "Kerwhap!"

The driver saw some traffic new,
And gave the brakes a punch,
Into the air Duke swiftly flew,
And almost lost his lunch.

Now a stretch on the winding side,
A series of sharp turns,
Duke hit the walls - a rocky ride -
Starting to get wood burns.

It seemed to Duke the miles did flit.
"This day's not in clover."
A sudden thought saw panic hit,
"Lord, don't let's turn over!"

How nudge the driver, dumb up-front?
That was the main issue.
"Aha," cried Duke, "Here's a neat stunt.
"A flag of white tissue!"

Out came the white, to Duke's delight,
And started trailing back,
The paper was tough (yes, truly rough!)
With wind, there was no slack.

Outback it slunk, it ended up,
On the cheek of a cop.
Down went the donut and the cup,
"That driver has to stop!"

On came lights, the truck pulled aside.
Asked the cop, much abused,
"An answer I want now! Don't hide!
Was that white paper *used*?"

From the shack whooped a grateful shout:
"Enough! It's made me wheeze!
"A lesson learned to all I'll flout,
"Next time, first steal the keys!"

*Mohylek at Polish Wikipedia*

# 8. QUANDARY IN THE CAMPGROUND

## (OR MY KINGDOM FOR A QUARTER)

*Who hasn't misread a sign once or maybe even twice?*

Pedro & Jane were parked in the camp,
After a long day out on the trail.
Their rig worked well though a bit basic,
With a bath being done from a pail.

But the campground had a better way,
Over there yonder were some showers,
In those structures with the metal roofs,
Right there with those pines and pink flowers.

With his sack of necessary gear—
Soap, towel, deodorant, and shampoo,
Pedro said adios for now to Jane,
And strolled over to the shower and loo.

To start the shower it took four quarters,
So, he slid them in to begin the game,
Then on came hot water – ooh, that felt good –
As it nicely soaked his sweat-laden frame.

"Ahh," said Pedro, as the water streamed down,
"A hot shower's much better than a creek,
After a busy day out on the trail,
Where the old bod takes on a strong reek."

He scrubbed his body parts with vigor,
With the bar of soap in full action,
Then on to his hair went the shampoo,
With fluffy foam gaining full traction.

"Huh? What the heck's goin' on now?"
Said Pedro, with a strong curse and wince,
"Why did that water shut off,
Just when I was ready for the rinse?"

He'd been having such a fine scrub,
He'd forgotten the timer was skipping,
Then came a click, with the result,
His water supply was barely dripping.

So, there he stood all soapy,
But his pouch was right there with the dough,
Just slide in four more quarters,
And once more, that hot water would flow.

So swiftly he slid in the first,
Then the needed second and third more,
Now dig once more into that pouch,
To grab up that quarter number four.

But no four was there – oops, no water—
So, from the stall, he stumbled, with a scoff,
As he stood there all covered with soap,
Thinking what to do now to get rinsed off.

Stumbling to the sink, he turned on that faucet,
Not a flow, but at least maybe a fix,
And, after a time, scooping water by hand,
He grumbled, "Next time, I'll stick to the cricks."

He got the soap off but made quite a mess,
Inspected his frame, yes now newly clean,
Wait, the mirror now showed a second face—
"Oops, what's she doin' here in the men's latrine?"

With towel hastily gathered 'round his waist,
Pedro said, "Ma'am, nice to see you, of course,
"But what are you doing here in my john,
Which, for us gents, is our bathing resource?"

"Not so much," she pleasantly replied,
"Thought I'd step into the facilities,
With the entrance sign reading 'Women,'
Where we ladies use our abilities."

"Oh no," gasped Pedro, looking chagrined,
And gathered his duds to make his amends,
With two lessons ingrained in his head,
"Bring more quarters and make sure it says 'MEN'S,'"

# 9. TWO WOMEN ON THE MOVE

As the urge hit Selma—it showed on her face—
She said to chum Tess, "Let's pick up the pace.
I had too much coffee—it's letting me know—
I'd better find quickly someplace to go."

But where can we go? Where might be a loo?
"Don't know but let's move, I've got to go too."
Oh, look over there - those two little huts,
Two havens all set for two little butts.

So, they dashed to the privies ending their flight.
Selma took the left hut, Tess grabbed the right.
Thank heaven for these privies so finely placed.
Two near-disasters will soon be erased.

Then that right door re-opened as Tess dashed back,
Now out darted Selma from the left shack.
Moaned Selma, "That porta-can's full to the brim."
From Tess, "The scent in here's totally grim."

"Not only that, but my desire did taper,
When a quick peek showed it had no paper,"
Shaking her head, Selma said "This is no treat,
"Look, on this one, there's not even a seat!"

So those huts were losers, but what's the next choice?
Their bladders were shouting not to rejoice.
Their eyes revealed panic as options weren't clear.
Zero hour was nigh, relief nowhere near.

"I have it," said Selma, "Let's exit this turf,
And calmly (but swiftly) head to the surf."
Thus, into the water went this perked-up team,
Chaos averted with this clever scheme.

So now when you see on a stroll by the shore,
Selma and Tess showing panic no more,

One factor you'll note as they wander their routes,
They always are wearing their bathing suits.

*Source: Tom's personal picture files*

# 10. YOU DON'T WANT TO BE THERE WHEN THE BLACK WATER BLOWS

*Many folks nowadays hit the road, often driving RVs (Recreational Vehicles) or pulling trailers. A required action is to drain the tanks that collect the water (and other deposits). Not always an easy task.*

Life out on the road has its real pleasures,
Being self-sufficient is one of life's treasures,
And as every RV owner knows,
You don't want to be there when the Black Water blows.

An RV, you see, has two vital tanks,
And they serve as two very special banks,
The Grey holds the nice water from the sinks,
The Black, the other stuff that sort of stinks.

So, when those two tanks start to get full,
The last thing you want is flow in the hull,
It won't serve you well to groan or grump,
Just look for a station in which to dump.

Now the process is really quite clear,
And it usually starts back in the rear.
Just hook up the drain hose to one tank,
Then pull that valve out and let that stuff crank.

At the dump station with my Dolphin,
Draining the tanks and thinkin' 'bout some golfin',
When next to me pulled in a huge rig,
With a driver who sorta' looked like a prig.

He was wearing a spotless jumpsuit,
Which would soon become definitely moot,
To the back end of this bus, he strode,
To dump his waste tanks in the usual mode.

The first task is to make the hose ends connect,
It's a simple task—no need to reflect,
One end to the black tank, the other the drain,
Give it a good twist, not really much strain.

"Now Zeke," came the sweet voice from inside,
"Finish up quick, got some burgers to be fried."
"Be right there,' said Zeke, 'Just get 'em set.
"I don't want to get my nice new jumpsuit wet."

So, Zeke pulled the lever, then came a loud splat,
As the hose popped away right off the bat,
And with the pressure of a week's heavy load,
The fluids spewed swiftly out on the road.

Poor old Zeke was now in a desperate mess,
Must hook on that hose under major league stress,
His jumpsuit was splattered from bottom to top,
As he frantically flailed to keep from a flop.

But that surge of pressure made one thing plain,
Zeke's desperate measures would all be in vain
Whatever he tried seemed not to matter,
All manner of stuff continued to splatter.

By now I'd moved my clean Dolphin away,
Wanting to keep poor Zeke's problems at bay.
I tried real hard to stifle a chortle,
Watching him try to secure that portal.

Finally, the drenched chap made his connection,
Then peered in the mirror at his reflection.
His once spotless suit was not fit for lunch,
As the wife said, "Come in now-- it's time to munch."

But Zeke was perched on a nearby bench
Hosing himself down to scrub off the stench.
From top to bottom he sprayed and cursed,
"Of all my RV days, this one's the worst."

Well Zeke proved to be a resilient dude
As he headed up for burgers in the nude.
One question was, midst those dishes and pans,
Did Zeke remember to first wash off his hands?

So, the lesson for all to know forever,
Make that hose tight before pulling that key lever.
Because as most every RV owner knows,
You don't want to be there when the Black Water blows.

*Publicdomainphotos | Dreamstime.com.jpg*

# 11. JOEY TAKES A NOSE DIVE

*Many outhouses have multiple holes for sitting,*
*thus accommodating the different sizes of the sitters.*

Gertie and Clyde had a regular family fray,
Three generations were gathered there on this day.
And when that nature's call would hit one of the pack,
It meant a trip out back to that little old shack.

Their shack was of the deluxe design feat,
With three holes to choose from in the seat.
Each hole sized for whoever'd encamp,
From kid to Ma to broad ol' Gramp.

Six-year-old Joey headed out on his tour,
Of the need to go, he was totally sure.
He arrived quickly at that functional abode,
Ready to make use of that waiting commode.

The smallest circle was well fit for his rear,
But this time, he just gave it a passing sneer.
He pranced past the mid one and flipped up the third lid,
The one Grandpaw said was off-limits to a kid.

Joey eyed that large hole and puffed out his chest.
"To heck with Gramps, I'm giving this one a test."
He undid his britches and bared his teeny buns,
"Why only the big butts? Why not us little ones?"

He breathed a smug sigh of awaiting pleasure,
After all, this would be his moment of leisure.
Then as he was almost perched on that grand place,
He started to slip through that large open space.

His legs headed up, and his bare rump slipped down,
And he started sliding toward that pit of renown.
Oh no!" howled Joey as he saw his new path
Heading him downward toward a less than fun bath.

His still-moving frame was almost clear through,
It looked like a no-hope drop in the stew.
But fate stepped on in (jolted by Joey's hoots?)
And the lid toppled down and captured his boots.

Now Joey's drop halted as he hung upside down,
Putting a hold, maybe short, on his path to drown.
Now he'd need a quick rescue, that need was real clear,
And he croaked, "Help, somebody! Get me out of here!"

But when met with silence, his fate seemed assured,
So, he screeched some more and –what's that? – something stirred!
Then Joey was startled as a rooster darted out,
"The last thing I need, old Chaser flitting about!"

Chaser, the top rooster, loved many a hen,
The shack was his special tranquility den.
With a rotted hole so he could get in and out,
He'd perch on a beam and his own talent he'd tout.

Chaser did not like someone messing up his peace,
Now his aim was to get this other's hoots to cease.
So, he raced back and forth outside the shack,
Crowing and cackling that made the hens step back.

Picking the weeds over in the tomato patch,
Even Grandpaw Clyde's old ears couldn't help but catch
The sound of that rooster over by the small house.
"Knock it off!" he said, "I'm going to shut up that louse!"

As he neared the hut, he heard other wailing,
"My gosh," said he, "That sounds like Joey's railing!"
It came from inside and was loud like a loon,
Then he opened that door with the crescent moon.

And he saw the closed lid on his own reserved space:
"I see two small boots, but where the heck's his face?"
The shouts from below confirmed that Joey was caught,
And that his efforts to escape had come to naught.

Clyde grabbed the boots and thought before pulling them up,
"Now don't be too hasty, he's a frisky young pup,
"Maybe let him drop, 'cause he'll sure have excuses,
"Teach him a lesson to watch which hole he uses."

But as a Gramp, he knew rescue was in order,
And he lifted that large lid right from its border,
Out came young Joey, heading up from the rubble,
Overjoyed that Gramps had saved him from big trouble.

The tyke flopped on the floor with a sigh of relief.
Chaser was still crowing, as he'd been the true chief.
When Joey grabbed him, Gramp said "Take care you little lug,"
Said Joey, "I'm now his fan, giving him a big hug!"

On visits now, Joey takes Chaser a special treat.
And when the shack calls, does he skip that Grandpaw seat?
No, but now he secures a rope tight with a wrench,
To make sure he stays away from that lurking stench.

# *12.* RODNEY DROPS THE GOODS

*For many of us, using the outhouse is not a skill we've honed.*
*Sometimes problems occur, requiring solutions we've not thought of before.*

At the Annual International meeting
The techies had gathered from all around,
With the theme of "Let's get back to the basics,"
And the location the grand old Fairground.

Rodney was having a fine time on the tour.
The guide had nicely enlightened them all.
The lunch was just fine, if a bit too much spice,
And all agreed they were having a ball.

But then he felt that old familiar signal,
That notice that says "Get a move on, Jack,"
Yes, time for a rapid perambulation
To that essential old shack out in back.

So back he perambled and opened the door
With that small sliver of moon on the front.
A one-holer it was, ready for action,
So, Rodney sat and proceeded to grunt.

After a bit, his business was concluded,
So' Rodney arose to pull up his trous.
But then a loud kersplat heard from down below
Caught his attention and gave him a rouse.

As Rodney was reconnoitering his parts
A peek past the seat caused a woeful groan,
When he saw resting amidst the fragrant murk,
What else but his all-important cell phone.

Having that durn thing slip right off from his belt
Left Rodney feeling like a clumsy lout.
But a major concern was firmly pressing:
What means could he use to scoop that phone out?

Rodney felt he had but one course of action.
To reach down with care and give it a snag.
So, with his left hand firmly squeezing his nose,
He stretched his right below for a quick bag.

When Rodney felt that pungent brew on his paw,
He gave a snort but still had to grab it.
But as he curled his hand round that slip'ry phone
His Rolex watch slipped off like a rabbit.

How could he let this pathetic stuff happen?
"You're just plain stupid," was his own retort.
With total disgust, he peeled off his jacket,
And into the stew, there went his passport.

Now Rodney was shaking his head in disgust
"As a good engineer, just got to think."
So, he leaned on over to reconnoiter
And his pocket protector hit the drink.

Now it was one thing to lose a cell phone
And you could buy a Rolex there or here.
But losing a pocket protector was rough,
As its load was your techie's vital gear.

"This is totally absurd," lamented our chap,
One more idea popped into his tup.
"What if I use my pants, still hanging around,
And reach on in and just scoop it all up?"

So, he tied a knot at the end of one leg,
And leaned in with care as his last resort,
And very cautiously did collect that phone,
Protector, Rolex, and even passport.

'Twas a happy Rodney that slipped back the goods,
And rejoined the group with little more fuss.
But the driver said, "Not with these pants of yours,
No way are you getting back on this bus."

# THE USUAL

There once was a chap name of Blue
Who oft hoisted many a brew,
Then moaned "My bladder's weak,
I've got to take a leak,
Quick point me the way to the loo."

# 13. OUTHOUSE BLUES

*Making use of your personal outhouse
can be a relaxing experience... maybe.*

On a pleasant morn, with the sun just born,
Bill Jones took a stroll out back.
'Twas a frequent jaunt to a fav'rite haunt,
Just a little old rustic shack.

Bill's mood did soar as he opened the door,
Unique with its crescent moon.
He tipped the lid, and on he slid,
While whistling a happy tune.

As he settled in, it was still within,
A place for meditation.
His cares untaxed, his stress relaxed,
To quiet contemplation.

His eyes were closed, he almost dozed,
And a grunt he did emit,
His vision blurred, his innards stirred,
As he then began to... grit.

Then he heard a rasp, and he woke up fast
When the boards began to crack.
His eyes came wide, and he grabbed the side,
His throne came under attack.

With a sudden drop, it went kerflop
Into that fragrant stew.
And down went Bill – Wow, what a thrill!
As airborne, he now flew.

"It's looking grim; I cannot swim,
"This day may be my last.
"Where is the sun? I am undone!"
Bill's life before him passed.

Dreading the splash into that mash,
Bill felt there was no hope.
Now near the murk, he felt a jerk.
A hook his belt did grope.

And there he hung, above the dung,
That hook had stayed his fate.
He took a breath. Whew! Not yet death,
But too soon to celebrate.

What can he do? What avenue
Can free him from this mess?
Is there a tool? He needs renewal
To bring him fast success.

A thought now clear brought Bill some cheer,
No need to hold his bladder!
And as he cheered, insight appeared,
"What's needed is a ladder!"

No more remorse, just find a source,
Some means to allay his fears.
Aha, what's this, that tool of bliss,
An old catalog from Sears!

Yes, there's the fix, page ninety-six,
That ladder with the flair.
With that in place, he could save face
And climb up to fresh air.

But how to call out to the mall,
Since Bill was all alone?
With hand, he felt along that belt,
And pulled out his cell phone.

Here came the crew, o'er to the loo,
The ladder they put in place.
To our man Bill, it was a thrill,
Relief from odious space.

So filled with cheer, he bought the beer,
The plaudits he did divvy.
And all still say, 'twas one fine day,
When Bill climbed from the privy.

# *14.* GETTING STRAIGHT POOP FOR THOSE SPECIAL SEATS

*Press item: U.S. Military pays $6000 per toilet seat*

The Senator was outraged when his aide showed him the costs.
"Surely that can't be true! You must be a decimal point off."
"No, sir, $6000 per seat was in the contractor's bill."
"Well, that much for one toilet seat is enough to make one scoff."

"And now it's made the headlines and my constituents are irate,
How could our Air Force spend six thou for one crummy seat?
So, clarify to me how that outrageous cost was achieved,
To make each seat that expensive had to be some mean feat."

"Is that throne made from rare marble or perhaps even of gold,
Or was the design tailored specially fit for use by a duke?
What the heck was in that contract that drove those charges so high?
Now the taxpayers are spouting that's enough to make them puke."

"Or is it trimmed in muskrat fur or warmed with solar power?
Then maybe each seat was specifically carved from precious teak,
Or are they bullet-proof to protect buns from sniper's attacks?
Or radar-protected so no enemy could sneak a peek?"

"And I'll bet they didn't hire from the regular labor force,
But artisans from the old school, so each is a work of art,
Wait, I'll bet it's in the Environmental Protection Act,
With output to be recycled plus a filter for each fart."

"Did they include hi-fi to help fighters enhance their relief,
Or with spigots to give each producer their own slug of rum?
Or perhaps—I'm reaching now—do these adjust to the sitter,
To add comfort by shaping the top to fit each person's bum?"

"Well," said the inquisitor, "Now I'm definitely pooped,
This search is exhausting, and my energy is nearly drained,
Go off and bring me numbers to get the press off my back,
And I'll have answers so my voters might be a bit restrained."

A day later, the numbers expert came back with the story.
"Sir," he said, "We've found what added to the liability.
It's a line buried in contract section 24 C9,
To place deluxe toilet seats in each Senator's facility."

*Usually, the outhouse has only one or two roles, but then they might fill other essential tasks (fill might not be the proper term).*

*Kim Howell/Shutterstock.com*

# 15. MY KINGDOM FOR A SEAT

*You may have mastered the skills required to use the outhouse in your neighborhood. But when traveling to new exotic places, those skills may need tweaking.*

PUT YOUR RIGHT FOOT ON...

Mabel and Earl were on their first tour abroad,
Dropped into Paris, strolled along the Seine,
Snickered in Florence while admiring David,
In Copenhagen chatted with a Dane.

They'd done their homework before heading off,
Read how to do it on ten Euros a day,
Found out if it's a pension or Gasthaus,
Where to sip der bier und den where to go pray.

Got enlightened from the Travel Channel,
Found the latest hot tips off the Internet,
Had a guide to keywords in ten countries,
Though it got tough with changes in alphabet.

But one vital instructional tip,
That for sure seemed to be woefully writ',
Was how to use a facility,
That would baffle a Yank if not a Brit.

When the time came to answer nature's call,
Whether the call was to tourist or thief,
The first requirement to be satisfied,
Was to find that special room for relief.

The guidebook had a translation chapter,
For asking, "Donda esta el bano?"
Or "Dove si trova la toilette,"
And they'd work well for Indian or Anglo.

Mostly they were standard routine,
Understood by a Yankee, Scot or Greek,
Step in, sit down and do your task,
Though the paper might scratch a tender cheek.

But on others, Earl found a different style,
One that meant squatting was the required mode,
The reason was it was missing a seat,
"What numskull invented this stupid commode?"

Earl was baffled about how to function,
If you can't sit down when you certainly must,
Even back on the farm, that house out back,
Had a place to park butt right there in the dust.

Earl did not have much time,
To explore a batch of suggestions,
"To squat or not to squat?"
That was not among the key questions.

Then that old ditty came to mind,
Put your right foot on (if you can find the place),
Make sure it's firmly settled, then
Put your left foot on atop that other space.

Now with feet planted it was time to proceed,
Earl dropped his drawers and went into the lurch.
"Aagh! Some unused muscles are feeling the strain,
They're moaning strongly from this torturous perch."

With task now completed, Earl creaked back on up,
Just one more task – all this hassle rankles—
So, he poked the flush button, once he found it,
And water surged up over his ankles.

"How was it, Earl?" asked his lady buddy,
"Did it cause a problem, or were you able?"
Earl, holding back a snicker, slyly said,
"Should be a piece of cake for you, dear Mabel."

# 16. DUCK & COVER

*In the military, rank has its privileges, and peonage has its costs.*

A detail not revealed in Gunga Din,
That classic tale about those chaps in a fight,
Over there in Asia, struggling to win,
Was, when you had to go, where was the darned site?

Well, most of the time we weren't too picky,
Just grab a bush nearby and give it a spray,
Or maybe squat to deposit a quicky,
Then out of the trenches and back to the fray.

Or sometimes when we returned from the front,
There they had those little houses called privies,
Where you could go sit whether tall or runt,
And no bushes there to poke through your skivvies.

After the bushes, these were mighty fine,
Though you'd have to smack spiders that here would lurk,
But one problem would sure ripple our spine,
And we'd curse the builder as a total jerk.

You see these privies had a second story,
Floor one was for privates to do their duty.
Floor two was where big shots could spout their glory,
And Captains could flop down and count their booty.

"So what?" you say, and maybe that's good flair,
Except floor two's seat was above first's housing,
So, if the Captain unloaded his ware,
The private's head would get a nasty dousing.

Thus, as we peons sat doing our thing,
We had to be constantly upward staring,
In case the rank above started a fling,
And was settling in with buttocks baring.

If we'd relaxed into a contemplative mood,
And failed to see those cheeks displayed up there,
A buddy seated near might intrude,
And shout a warning to move fast and beware.

Nothing would arouse us like that loud bray,
To a wild shift like leaving an ex-lover.
Those words are etched into our brains today,
As for many who've moved to "DUCK AND COVER!"

*Sue Smith/Shuttershock.com*

*This official service structure was designed so that the Colonels were happy to climb the short steps, and the Corporals didn't have to climb at all—they just had to duck.*

# 17. SKIP TO MY...WHAHHH???

*A pleasant warble makes life easier...in certain ways.*

Randy was a jolly old Brit,
With a flair for a lively tune.
When trekking to that shack out back,
He'd liven his passage with a croon.

Most days it was his standard jaunt,
A stroll after some chips with marlin,
We'd hear "Skip, skip, skip to my loo,
Then "Skip to my loo, my darlin'."

Then sometimes after too many prunes,
Or partaking excess of the ale,
We'd hear "trot, trot, trot to my loo,"
And "If I'm too slow, hand me a pail."

After one big supper at the pub
When he ate gobs of bacon with beans.
The next day a heavy price was paid,
And cut short his chatting the Colleens.

His innards said no time to delay,
Quickly now make like a kangaroo
Just hop out fast to the WC,
While chanting "Dash, dash, dash to my loo…"

Our Randy was a versatile chap,
And he managed to look quite dapper,
As he chose the appropriate tune,
On his journeys out to the crapper.

# 18. WHEN YOU GET THE CLUE, WHAT'RE YOU GONNA' DO?

*The urge arrives faster as the years do too.*

As the years advance, for certain geezers,
The need for relief provides some teasers.
When you're six, it's real easy to hold it
But at sixty, it's time to just fold it.

So, you're standing in that line at the bank
When that urge hits and you know it's no prank.
You pretend it's no more than a passing need,
And appeal to the clerk to pick up some speed.

But the line's not moving and what's that worm?
And you're trying to hide that need to squirm.
Was it wise to leave DEPENDS on its wrapper,
As you split the line and dash for the crapper?

So, you say enough of fighting that near-miss,
Maybe not heeding those clues would be remiss,
The ones the body is sending you aren't lies,
Ignoring the alerts has proven unwise.

So, you adopt a rule to quit balking
When those urgency signals start talking.
It's like some spook appears and says boo.
When you get the clue, head for the loo

Or you're poking that laptop at the shore,
And you want to tune that job a touch more,
Stop quibbling about the pro and con,
Just head on over to that porta john.

When you're tooling along out on the highway
And you sipped too much java at that café,
Don't take too long to park that nifty Chivvie,
Pull off to the side and hop in that privy.

Should the urge hit during the rev's sermon
(Especially if she's spouting in German),
It's not the time to think about a quiz,
Head past the last pew and take a quick whiz.

If the brain's saying it's number one for you,
No need to wonder what if it's number two?
Get going now, or it might be number three,
Move right on out to that handy WC.

And remember that last jaunt to Cancun
When too much tequila made you a buffoon,
Did you swiftly recall the keywords to know?
"Donde esta el ban-co or el ban-yo?"

So, remember there's little time to quibble,
When you must prevent that unwanted dribble.
So, whether you're at the market, church or zoo,
When you get the clue, what're you gonna do?

**Notes to clarify important terms:**

- loo, toilet in Britain
- W.C. same (Water Closet)
- el baño, toilet in Mexico
- geezers, men obviously older than this poet
- pew, seats in church (with alternate meaning when discussing this subject)
- whiz, relieving oneself

# *19.* THE OUTHOUSE THAT POOPED OUT

*We need that outhouse but who put it right there?*

The neighborhood lads were chatting away,
Mainly moaning about no place to play.
They had a ragged ball team of sorts,
With streets and alleys for their fields and courts.

Sometimes they'd trek over to that nearby park,
And they'd pop flies and chatter often 'til dark.
But it was a bit too cluttered and rough,
With gadgets, slides, swings, and stuff.

"Wish this place had a real ball field,"
Frustrated team member Roscoe appealed,
"Right there's some turf where we could take our places,
It's already grassy, how 'bout a few bases?"

"Well, that would be great," pitcher Jimbo did say,
"And we sure as heck need a better place to play,
An actual ball diamond would be highly amusing,
Better by far than those streets we're now using."

"But," said catcher Ragman, clearly the hope to douse,
"Right in the middle is that doggonned outhouse,
And that's right where the shortstop would repair,
No way can we play with that outhouse right there."

"It's handy when he'd pop in there to flounder,
But it makes it real tough to pick up a grounder.
Or dash over and bounce his head off that crapper,
That would make for one real painful rapper.

"It'd be nice if we could just haul it away,
And with it gone, we'd have a neat place to play.
But it's a lot more than just a porta-potty,
Those concrete blocks give it mighty tough body."

"So," asked Jimbo, "What might be a solution?
Knocking it down would create much pollution
And even a tractor with lots of… ahem… poop,
Couldn't get that John out with a big ole scoop."

Off to the side mused outfielder True Grit,
Thinking about Grandpa's blasting op at the pit.
"What if," he thought, "We laid some smackers where they'd stay,
So, they'd blast that potty off and away."

With the dilemma unsolved, the team called it a day,
With a lot of frustration not going away,
And no way to make it work seeming close to tragic,
But to get that outhouse removed would take real magic.

Next day at the park – the field idea a hopeless pursuit—
Pitcher Jimbo glanced out, feeling a bit resolute,
"What the devil? Has my vision gone completely askew?
Or has that outhouse disappeared right from my view?"

And as they all gazed intently out toward the park lawn,
They all agreed the outhouse was totally gone,
With only a few holes in the dirt and sediment,
To remind them what had been a big impediment.

Ragman crinkled his lips behind his catcher's mask.
Knowing no one had gone to the mayor to ask,
"What if... Do you think?... Likely baloney..."
As he glanced over toward his outfielder crony.

"Grit," he asked slyly, "Wasn't that just a bit scary?"
"Who me?" Grit mildly replied at such a query,
"Why would you ever consider such fluff?
Just because Gramps knows how to use that stuff."

"Oh, right," said Ragman, grinning with some game,
"Must have been a sudden twister that came,
And who cares as we now have a field on call,
And our team will get ready to hear 'Play ball!'"

So, the kids' team was delighted with this new situation,
Though neighbors spent time with definite irritation,
Grumbling that this method was maybe not so wise,
With Sears catalog papers raining down from the skies.

# 20. BIG BUNS STUCK UP THERE

*Riding those airline planes means some
situations are different from riding the rails.*

Yes, I am a fairly ample dude.
Eating well is a favorite pursuit,
And yes, eating often is my style,
More likely, spuds than veggies or fruit.

Now this airline has a new rule,
When you check in, they bring out the scale,
And if we measure 300 plus
An extra charge is bound to prevail.

Sure, when I settle in on the plane
I flop over some on the next guy's seat.
Yes, he's got to tuck it in a bit,
But I paid more to fly, so why the heat?

And when the time arrives for relief
I head back to that small john in the rear,
True it's less a stride than a waddle,
Those next to the aisle grab hold of their beer.

Now the story I'm here to tell you –
A sad something that happened to me—
When I squeezed in that room in the back
And assumed my place for more than a pee.

Done mulling over life's big issues,
And unloaded last night's prunes and chili,
I poked that button to flush it down
And a major swoosh emptied the willy.

All done now and on to the next step,
Just lift myself up and on to my feet,
Except one big problem now appeared
I was sucked tight onto that goldarned seat!

Well, what to do to get off that can?
I leaned to the right, but no success rose,
Leaning left still kept me stuck real tight
How about a lean forward to touch my toes?

Whatever I did, nothing would work
Whether I'd wriggle, twist, push-pull or hump,
That toilet's vacuum had sucked me flat,
So, there I was, tightly stuck on my rump!

You skinny sorts don't know the problem
Stuck on your butt at 30,000 feet,
Us plumpish dudes really lack options
To remove our buns away from that seat.

Scratching my head and looking around
Maybe something could make like a lever,
The door was closed tight from outside help,
This is one complicated endeavor.

Wait, what's that gadget I see nearby?
Could that funny thing be the help I seek?
If I could poke it beneath my rump,
Would that wooden rod make the vacuum leak?

YAHOO! I heard that sought-after hiss,
When that vacuum's tight pull finally did end,
And as I heisted my ample self up,
I said a big thanks to that plumber's friend.

# A KEY QUERY

There was a maiden named Dottie,
Who imbibed more than one toddy,
She'd been partying in the street
And asked, while being discrete,
"Where the heck's the porta-potty?"

# 21. WHERE DOES SANTA GO?

*Now when you think about this fellow and his many required winter deliveries, this might be a question worthy of discussion.*

So, tell me again, Grampa, about that Santa guy.
You say he flies all the night long, all over the place,
And then he pops down chimneys; I don't know how nor why,
Leaves toys, grabs milk and cookies, then he's off like a race.

Well, Grampa, one thing puzzles me, it's just got me miffed,
When he's out there all that time, something I'd like to know,
Is hour after hour, unless he's smart or swift,
Just tell me please, how, when, and where does old Santa go?

I know what happens to me, and all the pals I know,
After slurping lots of milk 'n munching more'n one snack,
Is somewhere along the way we've just all got to go,
At school, in our john at home, or behind a bush out back.

I know I shouldn't let that stuff trouble me or you,
But I picture him with his fanny perched off the sleigh
And going number one or, my gosh, old number two,
As he flies over some poor little kid's dinner tray.

Whether it's us little kids or that old Kris Kringle
The teachers said not to leave a mess or pollute.
So, I'd hate to think he's peeing right on our shingle,
Or out over the rail doing a flying salute.

And what about the TP? Or corncobs in the woods?
You taught us to flush or bury the residue.
We've all learned just how and where to get rid of the goods,
But it still baffles me, just what does Santa do?

Grampa put on his thinking look, so he wouldn't flub,
"Well Joey, young laddie, since you put me on the spot,"
Tilting his head a bit and giving his chin a rub,
"I can tell you about how Santa uses a pot."

"When he's laid out those gifts, there's no time to say hooray,
He just tweaks his nose and poof; he's back up with his bag.
And when that urge hits Santa, he just can't stop that sleigh,
No time to dawdle, nor read the North Pole Daily Rag.

"You see, what they show of that jolly chap and his team,
Is the front part of the sleigh, with lots of toys in back,
All colorful and neat or at least so it would seem.
But what you don't see is the sleigh towing a small shack.

"The door has a slot, and there's a vent out from the top.
And inside is a one-hole spot on which he can perch,
So he won't need some person's house for that crucial stop,
(Even with warm seats, smooth paper and late news to search).

"That outhouse in the rear is Santa's private potty,
A very important part of the whole entourage.
A tweak of nose, a quick sit, and a refreshed body,
While the reindeer go off toward the next roof or garage.

"So, Grandson, now you know how Santa has worked it out."
Perched on his dear grandpa's lap, Joey nodded just so,
"Now I see that he uses that shack he hauls about.
But Grampa, wait a minute, then where does *Rudolf* go?"

*Tom's Personal Photos*

# TITILLATING TALES *from the* OUTHOUSE

## OTHER SPICY TALE

*This is a set of poetic tales that do not specifically involve that little house out back.*

# 1. IS THERE ANY HOPE?

Frank and Vickie are a well-matched pair,
With years of connubial bliss,
Except for those issues that keep popping up,
Where one would cheer, the other'd just hiss.

Frank was perturbed as he sat on the john,
When his paper grab came to a stop,
He expected to pull from the bottom,
But no, this tissue came off the top.

Vickie!" he roared, "You've done it again,
You put the new roll on upside down,
It clearly is smoother to pull from below,
Not from the top!" he says with a frown.

"And please turn up that thermostat
It's freezing in here; I'm cold to my gut."
She keeps the house cool; he likes it warm,
That's not so good when he has a bare butt.

Later they're taking the dog for a stroll,
Fifi, the poodle's a Vickie fave,
Frank grumbles since he'd rather hear
A Rottweiler named Sinister rave.

At dinner, she's sipping her wine,
Gently sampling the white in her glass.
She watches her spouse slurp down his brew.
"Swilling from that can is so low class."

After supper, as he prefers to call it,
She relishes watching the stars waltz,
While during the breaks Frank clicks
To see who's enjoying the Cubs' faults.

"Where shall we go?" as they head out for lunch,
She's thinking that lovely French place,
But soon is shaking her head
As he drives into a Hooters parking space.

They're checking for the next night's concert,
"Light opera," hums Vickie," Maybe those winds."
While Frank's getting enthused about
The Country Yodelers or Cajun Skins.

Again, back home, Vickie heads for the john
And soon sends a snort on out to her spouse:
"Will you ever learn to put the toilet seat down?
Can't you be a gent instead of a louse?"

Frank mulls that over a moment
Then righteously makes his defense,
"Since I wee far more than I whomp
Keeping it up makes much more sense."

History tells us that couples often fuss,
Even different tools they chose to grasp,
Antony always went with his sword,
While Cleo's final choice was her asp.

# A PLACE TO P(LAN?)

A keen general was old Genghis Khan,
He won battles from hither to yon,
The insight that saw him succeed,
Was to hop on down from his steed
And plan each move while perched on the john.

*Carol M. Highsmith, Photographer*

# 2. THE LEGEND OF EMILY MORGAN, THE HEROINE OF SAN JACINTO

*The Battle of the Alamo is one of the country's best-known historical tales, with the Mexican troops, led by General Santa Anna, defeating the U.S. defenders. Lesser known is the following battle with Santa Anna's troops going up against a Texas military led by Samuel Houston. The Texan team thought a subtle strategy might help their effort.*

It was a day of glory for the General
As he rode slowly into the town,
Enjoying the rich accolades of victory
Fitting for this man of high renown.

Santa Ana was relishing this day, as,
Those rebels had fought hard to defend.
The battles at the Alamo had been fierce,
But his troops had won out in the end.

Now another bunch of trouble was stirring,
At San Jacinto, another fight.
A ragtag bunch claiming the name of
Texans, Going up against Mexican might.

Their leader was a fellow named Sam Houston.
With Jackson, he'd fought battles way back,
Lately, he'd seemed more an Indian than
Texan. Yet there he was now leading this pack.

But putting the crunch on that batch of Texans
Could easily hold off for a while,
Santa Ana's troops might need some time to rest,
Relaxing to fit the General's style.

Now Santa Ana, though a good family man,
Was known to grab romance on the run.
So, when most any day's battles were over
It was time for a good night of fun.

For the General, it was often his habit
To choose a lovely maiden for play,
What better way to renovate his vigor
Than the joy of a roll in the hay.

And now with that Alamo mess concluded,
The General felt that urge for reward.
While eying maidens of various styles and hues,
A special one put spark in his sword.

Her look revealed she was likely a servant.
The General declared of no import.
"And what is your name," he asked this comely one.
"Emily" came her sparky retort.

She said Morgan was the name of her master.
Then, said the General with eye agleam,
"Emily Morgan, come 'sup with me tonight."
So, this lady joined the General's team.

Now the General had put in some heavy days,
And Emily's style had tweaked his urge.
So, he set his quarters on a nearby plain,
So eager was he ready to merge.

That night Emily shared well his bed and zest,
So, well, it stretched on to the next day.
With hardly either showing outside the tent,
They were wrapped up in intimate play.

Their passion extended to another night,
The tent shaking with each hearty ride.
His aides had not seen the General so taken,
And one more day of action inside.

But now the General's aides sounded an alert
"Sir, a battle is looming ahead,
"And we're not well placed out on this open plain."
(Where our leader chose to make his bed.)

"We should move our tents and troops away from here,
So, we're positioned to take up arms."
But the General replied, "I'm too busy now."
And headed back to Emily's charms.

Now Houston saw opportunity at hand,
And moved his troops to the better space.
Then he gave the word to charge that open line,
And the Texans roared out at full pace.

"Remember the Alamo!" was their loud shout,
As they attacked with rifle and lance.
Capturing Mexicans galore plus one tent
With one General in his underpants.

Was he a worn man as he stood defeated?
Was he chagrined as he passed his sword?
Did his dalliance with Emily prove unwise?
Did her efforts earn her a reward?

The San Jacinto win was the key event
That made Texas a nation that day.
And what of Emily who captured the General?
Rumors were heard that she'd moved away.

Now with her name on a San Antone hotel,
Was she a tart or woman of fame?
Who was the real Yellow Rose of Texas?
Say, was Emily Morgan the name?

# 3. KC AT THE BAR

*We all know the best guy at the bat was that Casey dude?*

It looked extremely rocky for the Budvuls' crowd so far.
The scores were zero-ten against the hustlers round the bar.
And when Fleming was rebuffed, and Magurski met a scowl,
A pallor creased the faces of the keen dudes on the prowl.

Some of the guys threw in the towel and headed off depressed.
But some hung 'round, hope springing still from that eternal breast.
Though up to now, "Get lost, you bums," was sadly the routine,
They knew that often chicks said yes, once KC hit the scene.

Now Flynn was getting twitchy, and the same was hitting Blake,
But the former's line was wimpy, and the latter's like an ache.
So, their stamina was running low as closing hour drew nigh,
And their hopes were fading fast since KC had not stopped on by.

But Flynn gave it another shot and struck out once again,
And Blake's well-traveled pitch failed to draw in a single hen,
Just as the lads were set to concede this night would score no goon,
Their spirits got a boost when KC strolled into the saloon.

Word quickly spread that a special stud had newly hit the scene,
The stirring hustlers felt the unstirred foxes shifting into preen.
Maybe now the ladies would be less inclined to them berate,
As in the game of hustle, they saw KC approach the plate.

Now the hopes of Flynn and Blake were aroused more than a bunch,
If KC could stir the gals, success for them was their hunch.
So, the fellows gave him a thumbs up and ordered two more brews,
Licking their chops as KC ambled toward a fine pair of stews.

KC entered the game with one of his well-polished lines,
But he showed chagrin when greeted with less than friendly signs.
"Your spiel's worn out," said one, "We've heard it all from your cronies,
Maybe we've been taken in, but now we know you're phonies."

*Wikipedia Commons*

"Well!" sniffed KC just a bit and moved on down the bar
With another well-honed line that had oft-made him a star.
But one unstirred lassie said it was time for his act to stow,
Making it clear there was no room here for his tired oats to sow.

Flynn and Blake perceived their stirred-up chances swiftly sinking.
What chance had they if their clean-up hitter came up stinking?
Their hopes were totally squashed when one more fox called him a lout.
Tonight, there's no joy in Budvuls', mighty KC has struck out.

# 4. SATURDAY BATH ON THE FARM

Out on the farm on a Saturday night,
We hauled water from the well way down the path.
With a bucketful balanced on each side,
This was the night for that ritual known as the weekly bath.

No easy task, hauling those heavy pails,
Then onto the wood-burning stove and into the ready pot.
Right beside there was the round metal tub,
with a rough brush, rag, and bar of lava soap, the whole darned lot.

Mom and grandma were the matrons-in-charge,
Getting the next kid into the tub, half-filled with warm water.
Off went our duds and into the tub, we went,
Made no difference whether a grandkid, cousin, son, or daughter.

Then we sat in that old tub on the floor,
With Mom soaping your ears and giving your back a scrub and scratch,
And grandma dips hot water from the pot,
That warm pour on your skin is a feeling no shower can match.

All scrubbed clean now, your turn was over,
Up, you stood and grabbed a towel to dry off before you got cold.
Standing on the floor, naked as a bird,
Modesty is not a problem, not when you're just six years old.

But no hanging around, our time was done,
You doffed your duds and headed out while sister Jean headed in.
Out you went to the family room,
Where near the pot-bellied stove, kinfolk played canasta or gin.

Was there an order to the weekly bath?
I don't recall, but there was virtue in getting in early,
The first ones in got the freshest water,
And then—hooray—you didn't have to follow Uncle Curly.

—Published in 2015 Oasis Journal

# 5. I NEVER PEED IN THE POOL

In my hometown, summer meant hitting the pool.
For us kids, it was many a splash and a flop.
Some could swim well, and others were dog paddlers,
A few swam underwater while most stayed on top.

One day the lifeguard pair, Buck and Rosie,
Rounded up our gang to give us some flack.
"Kids," said Buck, "We have a question to ask."
"Oh, what would that be?" we queried right back.

"We watch you all carouse out here for hours,
With summer nearly done and heading back to school,
We're baffled that you never hit the john,
Are you sure you're not going right here in the pool?"

Well, no one had ever asked us about that,
As I'm standing there soaked, trying not to drool,
"Well," I said, "I don't know about the others,
But I sure know I never peed in the pool."

"And so you'll know I wouldn't fib to you,
I'm showing how we Cub Scouts solemnly swear
That on my honor my answer is true,
With my fingers displayed and hand in the air."

Now lifeguard Rosie chose to get in on the act
And asked my chum Kat, sitting high up on a stool,
"How come we never see you going in for a break?"
"Well, same here," huffed Kat, "I never peed in the pool."

"OK," said Buck, giving chum Spike a dubious look,
"What's your line, kid? You gonna make like a dumb mule?"
"Geeze," sniffed Spike, giving him back an offended glare,
"I wouldn't kid you; I never peed in the pool."

Now Rosie switched over to her detective hat,
"That's so nice, Spike," then went on the attack.
"But when you're giving us such a heartfelt response,
Why are your fingers crossed behind your back?"

Spike, showing offense, defended his body style,
"You're just like our teacher, with her look aimed to fright,
And as I told her, it's just a medical state,
My fingers get swollen, so I must squeeze them tight."

Rosie gave Kat another skeptical look
"Young lady, something was strange about your reply,
When your eyes peered away at something above."
Said Kat with a grin, "A bird up there caught my eye."

Buck turned to me and said he'd been a Cub Scout too,
Stating, with a glare suspicious to the core,
"Our pledges were done with the right hand, not the left,
And we proclaimed showing two fingers, not four."

"Well, there's a simple explanation," said I,
While giving him a sharp look of disdainful heft,
"When I swim, I hold my nose with my right hand,
So, when you grilled me, I forgot and raised the left."

So now you who are reading our tale of inquest,
Of lifeguards seeing if we'd broken some rule,
What's your story? Can you, as honestly as we,
Proclaim, "Heck no - I never peed in the pool!"?

# 6. TROUBLE AT THE MARKET
## (OR) YOUR ENGLISH LANGUAGE SUCKS

This English language is a strange one.
Very complicated.
Just when it looks like my lesson's done
It gets me cogitated.

Just listen to this pathetic tale,
From a journey to the store.
I wandered in looking for a sale
And got pitched out with a roar.

It seemed to be just a simple thing,
No big deal at all to me.
I asked the clerk in the produce bin
"May I please sir, take a pea?"

His face took on a disturb-ed look,
It was all a mystery.
He hustled me from the veggie nook,
"Out there's where you take your pee!"

But I marched back in to vent my spleen,
With him once more to speak.
"Why's it o.k. if I take a bean,
But not if I take a leek?"

In sweets, the clerks really made a lunge
Gasped like a pair of rookies.
They dashed off for a map and sponge
When heard, "I lost my cookies."

At meats, I must have made a sin,
They just howled and got real loose
When I queried with a friendly grin,
"Who will give me a big goose?"

Then over at the dairy section
They snorted with a wheeze,
Was it something about my question,
When I asked, "Who cut the cheese?"

This food verbiage gives me a tickle
Even dressed in my new garb.
The big boss said I'm now in a pickle
For making a big rhubarb.

He said "Be gone, and take your poodle
Don't mess with our Amanas.
Until you learn to use your noodle
You're driving us bananas."

So, they pitched me out – showed me the gates.
My words just met with curses.
Not even got to use my rebates,
Just went from bad to worses.

So back home I went to make my tea,
And cook from snitches and snatches.
The recipe books bewilder me –
I just make it from the scratches.

What's with these dumb English language words?
You can stick them in your ears!
It's simple, Hah! I give you the birds!
What's next? Get tossed from Sears?

The words I use create confusion,
Often in the State of Flux.
It thus brings me to one conclusion,
Yes, your English language shucks!

## 7. HOW SWEET THE AIR... GASP, COUGH, AGHHH

In this hectic world of rapid pace,
How lovely the little joys.
With relish, men unwind the chase
And again are little boys.

It's universal I suggest,
A deed that makes grown men flip,
In Peking, Chi or Budapest,
When some rascal lets one rip.

In workout togs or business suits
Or a crew waving paddles,
Guffaws greet those musical toots
Just like in Blazing Saddles.

The victims moan and loudly vent
At the scoundrel's loud release.
The guilty one looks innocent,
With a silent inner peace.

A stunt that's sure to spark some joy,
Gets an impish grin to start,
When in a crowded room he's coy,
And then cuts a sneaky fart.

Temptation brings forth evil thought,
When the crowd is unwary,
To send forth odor, he has brought,
Rank perfume that is scary.

Some cunning chaps look for chances
To wrinkle up some noses,
Then watch victims swap their glances,
Whoo! That scent sure ain't roses.

When the jerk behind the counter
Treats you much like sleaze,
It's playback time from your end
As you slyly cut the cheese.

The elevator's a sure place
That takes a special flair.
When all are jammed into tight space,
Some just love to foul the air.

At work, they're all in a meeting
When you sneak one so discrete,
Attention fast all is fleeting
Now point your finger at Pete.

See that bunch at the next table,
Gaily chatting while downwind.
Take advantage while you're able
Just fart, no need to rescind.

At the movie, the crowd's all a-whir,
The plot makes no one quit.
When a rank "whew" creates a stir,
Only you know who-dun-it.

There's that loudmouth on a cell phone,
Abusing your dining fun.
Such a pleasure to hear him groan,
From your well-aimed, potent one.

When that lout chomping the fritos,
Is knocking friends in the cast,
You call on last night's burritos
And disperse that crowd real fast.

On a bus just make one "Ca-Room,"
It'll drive the riders silly,
With some extraneous perfume
From last night's bowl of chili.

When at church the putrid fragrance
Gets all to wondering who.
One suspect gets many a glance
Of course, it's Pepe le Peu.

# CAPONE

One mean boss was that guy named Capone,
His decrees made some other crooks groan.
When planning his next big stink
He'd go sit where he could think
That small room where he mounted his throne.

# 8. GUYS DON'T PEEK
## WHEN BUSINESS CALLS

The well-known dude trekked into the room,
That one labeled as only for men,
Don Juan was famed for sexual conquests,
But this was purely basic, not sin.

Juan took his place at the two-stall spot,
And proceeded to undo his zipper,
Then out came his tool to do the job,
Soon a steady stream ran down the dipper.

A less-fancy dude strode into the room,
Waldo arrived to do his own thing,
He took his place at the second john,
The one right next to the make-out king.

Neither chap spoke even a word,
As they functioned away at their stalls,
No more than silence or a hum,
Just standard practice when duty calls.

Job done, Waldo regaled his waiting spouse,
"Hey, guess who I stood next to in there!
It was that Don Juan guy that makes the news,
Hot time with the ladies is his flair."

"We were just a couple of dudes,
During that time, as we partook."
"My Gawd!" she said, with a loud gasp,
"Tell me then, dear hubby—Did you look?"

Well, when Waldo heard that curious nudge,
He was taken more than a bit aback.
"Honey," he replied, "there's one firm rule –
To be a 'gent and clearly not a quack."

"That's not a place where we blab away,
We gaze ahead like we're at a brook,
And above all, there's that basic rule,
Whatever they do, guys sure don't look."

*It sure is nice when those porta-potties show up out there in unusual places (where and when your system might shout GO).*

*Karenfoleyphotography/Shutterstock.com*

# TITILLATING TALES
*from the*
# OUTHOUSE

## BACK TO THE OUTHOUSE

*The toilet, in its various styles, has been the subject of poetic tales from some of our most famous authors. Here are a few dandies.*

# 1. THE PASSING OF THE BACKHOUSE

By James Whitcomb Riley

*(Known as "The Hoosier Poet" Riley was the author of many poems during the 19th century.)*

When memory keeps me company and moves to smile or tears,
A weather-beaten object looms through the mist of years,
Behind the house and barn, it stood, a half a mile or more,
And hurrying feet, a path had made, straight to its swinging door.

Its architecture was a type of simple classic art,
But in the tragedy of life, it played a leading part.
And oft the passing traveler drove slow and heaved a sigh,
To see the modest hired girl slip out with glances shy.

We had our posey garden that the women loved so well;
I loved it too, but better still I loved the stronger smell
That filled the evening breezes so full of homely cheer,
And told the night—o'ertaken tramp that human life was near.

On lazy August afternoons, it made a little bower
Delightful, where my grandsire sat and whiled away an hour.
For there the summer mornings, its very cares entwined,
And berry bushes reddened in the streaming soil behind.

All day fat spiders spun their webs to catch the buzzing flies
That flitted to and from the house, where Ma was baking pies;
And once a swarm of hornets bold had built their palace there,
And stung my unsuspecting Aunt—I must not tell you where.

My father took a flaming pole—that was a happy day—
He nearly burned the building up, but the hornets left to stay.
When summer bloom began to fade and winter to carouse,
We banked the little building with a heap of hemlock boughs.

But when the crust is on the snow, and sullen skies were gray,
Inside the building was no place where one could wish to stay.
We did our duties promptly, there one purpose swayed the mind;
We tarried not, nor lingered long, on what we left behind.

The torture of the icy seat would make a Spartan sob,
For needs must scrape the flesh with a lacerating cob,
That from a frost-encrusted nail suspended from a string—
My father was a frugal man and wasted not a thing.

When Grandpa had to "go out back" and make his morning call,
We'd bundle up the dear old man with a muffler and a shawl.
I knew the hole on which he sat—'twas padded all around,
And once I tried to sit there—'twas all too wide I found,

My loins were all too little, and I jack-knifed there to stay,
They had to come and get me out, or I'd have passed away,
My father said ambition was a thing that boys should shun,
And I just used the children's hole 'til childhood days were done.

And still, I marvel at the craft that cut those holes so true,
The baby's hole, and the slender hole that fitted Sister Sue,
That dear old country landmark; I tramped around a bit,
And in the lap of luxury, my lot has been to sit,

But ere I die I'll eat the fruits of trees I robbed of yore,
Then seek the shanty where my name is carved upon the door.
I ween that old familiar smell will soothe my jaded soul,
I'm now a man, but none the less I'll try the children's hole.

*Note: This poem has long been in circulation, and there is disagreement as to whether Riley was the true author. It is also known by the title "The Old Backhouse."*

# 2. THE THREE BARES

By Robert Service

*(This author's humorous, poetic tales strongly hit the public during the late 1890's Alaskan Gold Rush. He continued with poems about other topics and places, many non-humor.)*

Ma tried to wash her garden slacks, but couldn't get 'em clean.
So she thought she'd soak 'em in a bucket of benzine.
It worked all right. She wrung 'em out, then wondered what she'd do
With all that bucket load of high explosive residue.

She knew that it was dangerous to scatter it around,
For Grandpa liked to throw his lighted matches on the ground.
Somehow, she didn't dare to pour it down the kitchen sink
And what the heck to do? Yet poor Ma just couldn't think.

Then nature seemed to give the clue as down the garden lot
She spied the edifice that graced a solitary spot,
Their Palace of Necessity, the family joy, and pride
Enshrouded in morning-glory vine, with graded seats inside.

Just like that cabin Goldilocks found, occupied by three.
But in this case, B-E-A-R was spelt B-A-R-E.
A tiny seat for Baby Bare, a medium for Ma,
A full-sized section sacred to the Bare of Grand Pa Pa.

Well Ma was mighty glad to get that worry off her mind
And heftin' up that bucket so combustibly inclined,
She hurried down the garden to that refuge so discrete,
And dumped the liquid menace safely through the center seat.

Next morning old Grandpa arose. He made a hearty meal
And smelt the air and said, "My gosh, how full of beans I feel.
Heh, heh, darned if I ain't as fresh as paint. My joy will be complete
With just a quiet session on the usual morning seat.

"Just smoke me pipe and meditate and maybe write a poem
For that's the time when bits of rhyme gets jiggin' in me dome."
He sat down on that special seat, slicked shiny by his age
And lookin' like Walt Whitman, just a silver-whiskered sage.

He filled his corncob to the brim, then tapped it snugly down
And chuckled, "Heh, what a perfect day, I reckon this the crown."
He lit the weed; it soothed his need, it was so soft and sweet
And then he dropped the lighted match clean through the middle seat.

His little grandchild, Rosaline, cried from the kitchen door
"Oh, Ma, come quick. There's something wrong. I heard a dreadful roar.
Oh, Ma, I see a sheet of flame. It's risin' higher and higher.
Oh, Mama dear, I sadly fear our comfort-cot's caught fire."

Poor Ma was filled with horror at them words of Rosaline.
She thought of Grandpa's matches and that bucket of benzine.
So down the garden geared on high, she ran with all her power
For regular was Grandpa and she knew it was his hour.

Then graspin' gaspin' Rosaline, she peered into the fire
a roarin', soarin' furnace now, perchance old Grandpa's pyre.
But as them twain expressed their pain, they heard a hearty cheer.
Behold, the old rapscallion's squatting in the duck pond near,

His silver whiskers singed away, a gosh-almighty wreck
With half a yard of toilet seat entwined about his neck.
He cried, "Say, folks, oh, did you hear the big blowout I made?
Heh, heh, it scared me stiff. I hope you-un's was not too much afraid.

Now I best be crawlin' out of this darn-gasted wet,
For what I aim to figure out is what the heck I et!

# 3. TOILET SEATS

## By Robert Service

While I am emulating Keats, my brother fabrics toilet seats,
The which they say are works of art, aesthetic features of the mart.
So exquisitely are they made, with plastic of a pastel shade,
Of topaz, ivory or rose inviting to serene repose.

Rajahs, I'm told, have seats of gold. They must, I fear, be very cold.
But Tom's have thermostatic heat, with sympathy your grace to greet.
Like silver, they are neon lit, making a halo as you sit.
Then lo! they play with dulcet tone a melody by Mendelssohn.

Oh, were I lyrical as Yeats, I would not sing of toilet seats,
But rather serenade a star—yet I must take them as they are.
For even kings must coyly own them as essentials as a throne.
So, as I tug, tug, tug the Muses teats, I envy Tom his toilet seats.

*Footoo/shutterstock*

# TITILLATING TALES
##### —— *from the* ——
# OUTHOUSE

## WILLIAM SHAKESPEARE

*Wikipedia Commons*

*And finally, we close out our epic outhouse tales, with memorable insights from perhaps the world's greatest poet, William Shakespeare, the Bard of Avon*

# 1. THE BARD HEADS FOR THE PRIVY

*Note: Purloined and slightly tuned from the works of Wm. Shakespeare, with help from Sir Thomas Leech*

It hit Bill as he eyed the spittoon,
That urging that just won't abate.
A pause, then "Better three hours too soon,"
—he said, "than a minute too late."

— Merry Wives of Windsor

In Stratford, it meant a stroll in rhyme
To that house, the Bard had to see.
Moving fast, musing, "I wasted time
—not good—and now time doth waste me."

— Richard II

Just then a fine odor made its claim
As he stepped swiftly from the street,
"Yes, a privy by any other name,"
The Bard observed, "would smell as sweet."

— Romeo & Juliet

Bill charged rapidly across the floor
In his need to swiftly get bare,
But first, he thumped hard on the door,
Asking, "Knock, knock, anyone there?"

—Macbeth

With silence returned, Bill whistled a tune
For sure, there's no need for a speech.
Flip open the door with that crescent moon
And head, "Once more into the breach."

—Henry V

I say, "this castle hath a pleasant seat."
Rustic, but it recompenses.
"The air nimbly and sweetly" doth entreat
"Recommends to our gentle senses."

— Macbeth

Decision first: "To pee or not to pee?"
Yes, indeed, that is the question.
"To sit, perchance to dream?" Why not, could be.
He seemed open to suggestion.

—Hamlet

Then up came his shirt and down went his hose,
"Come sit down, every mother's son."
No more delay, "Draw the curtain
close and let's all to meditation."

—Midsummer Night's Dream and Henry VI


In this place of bliss far from their wives
Not to any need one kow-tow.
Thus, "There's not a minute of our lives
Should stretch without some pleasure now."

—Antony & Cleopatra


Shhh, some wings a flutter overhead…
Is that perhaps something to fear?
Just bats, rats, and spiders—"O Wonder!
How many goodly creatures're here!"

—The Tempest


Then get down to business—"Now set the teeth"
(a groan) "and stretch the nostril wide."
Forsooth 'tis the time for serious relief,
"More matter with less art," he sighed.

—Henry V and Hamlet

But what if our production's deficient?
Do not fret—"If we fail, we fail."
Ah, success! The output proves sufficient.
"For this relief, much thanks." Regale!

—Macbeth and Hamlet

And now to end this operation,
"Ay, there's the rub," came from the pot.
The paper seems well past salvation.
A grumble, then "Out, out damn spot."

—Macbeth

Done now—"Brevity is the soul of wit."
Major needs have been all attended.
He fine-tuned his wardrobe to better fit,
Musing "This business is well ended."

—Hamlet, *Hamlet*

*And thank you, dear Bard, for letting*
*us peruse the relief requirement so well.*

**More Final Words from the Bard**

Truly **"All's well that ends well."**
It's always good when
**"The long day's task is done."**
And as we close that door with the quarter moon cut into it, and back into the world,
"Here is my journey's end, here is my butt, and the very seamark of my utmost sail."

As he wrote in
*All's Well That Ends Well,*
*Antony & Cleopatra,*
*and* **Othello.**

# TITILLATING TALES
### *from the*
# OUTHOUSE

## FOR THOSE WHO WANT TO SIT AND THINK

*Santeri Viinamaki*

*Other worthy, relevant, historic, and humorous tomes, of which there are many as the subject is a favorite of many authors, readers, and users.*

# SOME CLASSIC OUTHOUSE GEMS
## THREE-PLUS DECADES OLD

*CLEAN AND DECENT: THE FASCINATING HISTORY OF THE BATHROOM and the Water-Closet*
   Lawrence Wright. 2005 (original, 1960).

*GUEST REGISTER for the John*
   Orville Fenderlob. Konrom, 1977.

*OUTHOUSE HUMOR*
   Billy Edd Wheeler. August House, 1988.

*OUTHOUSES OF THE EAST*
   Sherman Hines and Ray Guy. Nimbus Publ. 1981.

*PRETTY PRIVIES OF THE OZARKS*
   Mahlon N. White. Democrat Publishing Co. 1975

*THE SPECIALIST*
   Chic Sale. Specialist Publ, 1929, 1956.

# MORE CURRENT OUTHOUSE DANDIES

*An Outhouse by Any Other Name*
    Thomas Harding. August House, 1999.

*Captain Underpants and the Tyrannical Retaliation of the Turbo Toilet 2000*
    Dav Pilkey. Scholastic, Inc., 2014.

*Great American Outhouse Stories: The Hole Truth and Nothing Butt*
    Patricia Lorenz. Infinity Publishing, 2013.

*Hidden Assets: Stories behind the Throne*
    Dori Hutson. Contemplation Publications, 1996.

*Little Outhouse in the Outback: Homesteading in Australia's Northern Territory*
    Chik Hylton, 2017.

*My Folks: Back to the Basics, A Treasury of Outhouse stories*
    Michele R. Webb, Editor. Capper Press, 1994.

*Nature Calls: The History, Lore, and Charm of Outhouses*
    Dottie Booth. Ten Speed Press, 1998.

*Ode to the Outhouse: A Tribute to a Vanishing American Icon*
  Foreword by Roger Welsch. Voyageur Press, 2002.

*Outhouses*
  Roger Welsch, Motorbooks Int'l, MBI, 2013.

*Outhouses of Alaska*
  Harry Walker. Epicenter Press, 1996.

*Outhouses of the West*
  Silver Cameron & Sherman Hines. 2000.

*Outhouses: Flushing Out America's Hidden Treasures*
  Londie Garcia Padelsky. Ostoecklem Publishing, 2005.

*Pete's Mighty Purty Privies*
  Aubrey Wynne. 2015

*The Compleat Loo. A Lavatorial Miscellany*
  Roger Kilroy. Victor Gollancz Publ., 1984 and Barnes & Noble Books, 1996.

*The History of Outhouses*
  Robert E Falk. CreateSpace Independent Publ., 2013.

*The Little House Out Back*
  George Borum. Nu-Art Pub, 2014

*The Outhouse Book*
  Ben Goode. Apricot Press, 1997, 2003.

*The Outhouse Papers: Country Humor and Trivia*
  Wayne Erbsen. Native Ground Music, 2001.

*There's a Porcupine in My Outhouse: Misadventures of a Mountain Man Wannabe*
  Michael Tougias. Capital Discoveries, 2002.

*Thunder, Flush and Thomas Crapper: An Encyclopedia*
  Adam Hart-Davis. Michael O'Mara Books, 1997.

*Toilets of the World*
  Morna E. Gregory and Sian James. Merrell Publishers, 2006.

# EVEN MORE OUTHOUSE EVENTS AND PLACES

BARNEY SMITH'S Toilet Seat Art Museum, San Antonio, Texas
https://www.roadsideamerica.com/story/6166

GREAT KLONDIKE INTERNATIONAL OUTHOUSE RACE, DAWSON CITY,
https://dawsoncity.ca/event/great-klondike-international-outhouse-race/

GREAT OUTHOUSE BLOWOUT, Penn's Store, Gravel Switch, KY
https://www.youtube.com/watch?v=XHIu_PYW2UM

GREAT SAPPHIRE VALLEY OUTHOUSE RACES, Cashiers, NC
https://cchikes.com/great-sapphire-valley-outhouse-races/

MUSEUM OF THE OUTHOUSE, Liverpool, Nova Scotia, Canada
http://www.rossignolculturalcentre.com/outhousemuseum.html

OUTHOUSE RACES AT SAGINAW, MI
https://www.mlive.com/news/saginaw-bay-city/2019/02/

SOUTH DAKOTA OUTHOUSE MUSEUM, Colome, SD
https://www.roadsideamerica.com/tip/1185

# HERE'S SPACE FOR YOUR POETIC NOTES

# ABOUT TOM LEECH

*Tom Leech, photo by Howard Bagley*

For many decades as an author, poet, and engineer, Tom has helped people improve their communication skills and success by applying the concepts from his books:

*How To Prepare, Stage & Deliver Winning Presentations,* 3rd Edition, released in 2004, was rated one of six "Top of the Class" books by Presentations Magazine.

*Say it like Shakespeare: the Bard's Timeless Tips for Communication Success,* 2nd Edition has been a top seller for speakers and speechwriters for almost twenty years.

His other books cover a variety of topics:

*Fun on the Job: Amusing and true tales from Rosie-the-Riveters to Rocket Scientists at a Major Aerospace Company.* is a compendium of anecdotes from his career as an engineer at San Diego's General Dynamics, Convair Division

*On the Road in '68: A year of turmoil, a journey of friendship* tells of his 'round-the-world travels to 27 countries in tumultuous year 1968.

*The Curious Adventures of Santa's Wayward Elves* with wife Leslie is an illustrated children's book.

His poems have appeared in many of his books and anthologies, including the Oasis Journal, Ageless Authors, *The Guilded Pen,* (the annual collection published by the San Diego Writers & Editors Guild,) *Heart of the Holidays,* and his Indiana hometown paper.

Wearing his weekend hat he is co-author, with GD colleague Jack Farnan, of *Outdoors San Diego: Hiking, Biking and Camping* (Premier 2004) and was longtime Editor of the Outdoors Forum for *San Diego Magazine.*

Visit his web site www.presentationspress.com for book details. Tom invites you to communicate with him via Facebook, Linked-in, and tomleech68@gmail.com e-mail.

# AFTERWORD

*You never know when you might need a porta-potty and appreciate it when you locate one where you thought it was not likely.*

*Michal Stipek/Shutterstock.com*

www.ingramcontent.com/pod-product-compliance
Lightning Source LLC
LaVergne TN
LVHW091535070526
838199LV00001B/68